COMPASSIONATELY
TRUTHFUL

COMPASSIONATELY TRUTHFUL

Finding Joy, Peace, And Love In Each Today

GERALD SUTYAK

XULON PRESS

Xulon Press
2301 Lucien Way #415
Maitland, FL 32751
407.339.4217
www.xulonpress.com

© 2021 by Gerald Sutyak

All rights reserved solely by the author. The author guarantees all contents are original and do not infringe upon the legal rights of any other person or work. No part of this book may be reproduced in any form without the permission of the author. The views expressed in this book are not necessarily those of the publisher.

Due to the changing nature of the Internet, if there are any web addresses, links, or URLs included in this manuscript, these may have been altered and may no longer be accessible. The views and opinions shared in this book belong solely to the author and do not necessarily reflect those of the publisher. The publisher therefore disclaims responsibility for the views or opinions expressed within the work.

Unless otherwise indicated, Scripture quotations taken from the New King James Version (NKJV). Copyright © 1982 by Thomas Nelson, Inc. Used by permission. All rights reserved.

Paperback ISBN-13: 978-1-6628-1822-6
Ebook ISBN-13: 978-1-6628-1823-3

Forward

WHAT IS COMPASSIONATELY TRUTHFUL? WHAT does this mean? How will this help in my life? How can I make "Compassionately Truthful" a reality in my life and in the lives of others? I was involved with helping people for many years, professionally and socially. I learned that being truthful with them was very beneficial by using the following words: "I will be honest with you, and I expect you to be honest with me." I chose, and still do, to live by these words. I will follow God's way, for He loves me and I know He will always be up-front with me. If I run from my problems then I am running from the truth, from our Heavenly Father. When one searches for answers alone, that individual does not understand the word wisdom. One can find all the knowledge in the world yet not have wisdom. Wisdom comes from Him and learning from Him. So I am very thankful that I have Jesus Christ in my life. He is always Compassionately truthful.

People will cause problems; regretfully, we will cause others and ourselves problems. God does not cause us problems. Therefore, we can move forward in the journey of life with Compassionate Truthfulness while finding peace and joy through love, His Love.

I have been through many sad/hard times and joyful/rewarding times. The way through the sad/hard times was seeking His peace, love, and joy. However, my selfishness stood in the way. Me, me, me, I knew what and how to get through my hurt, my pain. Yet, as I would complete each journey, I found that I was never alone. God was there the whole time through my tears of hurt, sadness, and loneliness. You see, I was concerned about me and not about the truth. When God's Wisdom guides us we do not seek the ME; we seek Him, the Truthful and Compassionate Father!

I heard "You'll Never Walk Alone" one day many years ago. The man singing it was Don Bartlette. This man had walked alone many times in his life. He had faced many trials and tribulations. Yet, when I heard him sing this song, I had tears of joy running down my face instantly. My heart reached out in prayer, thankful prayers, joyful prayers from hearing this man's journey in life.

When you walk through a storm:

> *Hold your head up high*
> *And don't be afraid of the dark.*
> *At the end of the storm*
> *Is a golden sky*
> *And the sweet silver song of a lark.*
> *Walk on through the wind,*
> *Walk on through the rain,*
> *Tho' your dreams be tossed and blown.*
> *Walk on, walk on*
> *With hope in your heart*
> *And you'll never walk alone*
> *You'll never walk alone.*
> **Oscar Hammerstein II**

My brothers and sisters, please walk with me as we seek healing through His truth and love.

Introduction

If I speak in the tongues of men or of angels, but do not have love, I am only a resounding gong or a clanging cymbal. If I have the gift of prophecy and can fathom all mysteries and all knowledge, and if I have a faith that can move mountains, but do not have love, I am nothing. If I give all I possess to the poor and give over my body to hardship that may boast, but do not have love, I gain nothing. Love is patient, love is kind. It does not envy, it is not proud. It does not dishonor others, it is not self-seeking, it is not easily angered, it keeps no record of wrongs. Love does not delight in evil but rejoices with the truth. It always protects, always trusts, always hopes, always perseveres. Love never fails. But where there are prophecies, they will cease; where there are tongues, they will be stilled; where there is knowledge, it will pass away. For we know in part and we prophesy in part, but when completeness comes, what is in part disappears. When I was a child, I talked like a child, I thought like a child, I reasoned like a child. When I became a man, I put the ways of childhood behind me. For now we see only a reflection as in a mirror; then we shall see face to face. Now I know in part; then I shall know fully, as I am fully known. And now these three remain: faith, hope, and love. But the greatest of these is love. *1 Corinthians 13*

Acknowledgements

First and foremost, I would like to thank our Lord and Savior Jesus Christ for all He has done for us. His forgiveness is where we begin to live for our Father, God! God has blessed me with so many true and giving friends! I am blessed by our Lord; and He alone has made it possible, through His Grace, that I am able to thank and acknowledge these blessed and gracious people.

My wife, Elizabeth (Liz), who encouraged me over and over to write this book and to continue to write about our Savior's place in our lives.Liz came to know me through something I wrote: "God's gift to me was life, and my gift to Him is what I do with His gift." In fact, Liz has, with the Lord's guidance, made my gift to Him grow!Liz also edited this book, and sometimes I received looks of "what are you trying to say in this ....." I Thank God for her fortitude and commitment; otherwise, there were some "oops" in my first few attempts that would not have been corrected, and the message would not have been as clear and consistent as we would have liked. Thanks, "Sweet Pea".

Rick, a preacher I met years ago, has become my brother in Christ. What a true and trustworthy Christian Rick is! While I might not always agree with Rick, he is compassionately truthful with me. His humor, if we want to call it that, is always there, whether I like it or not. Rick is just being Rick; no questions are allowed! Yet all who know him find his heart is about serving the Lord.Rick will not let you down; he serves our Great and Awesome

God with a compassionate truthfulness that we would like all mankind to adhere to, plain and simple! Thanks, Rick!

My sons, Jerry and Craig, a part of my life that is so full of blessings, continue to inspire me.God's plan has always been and will always be to follow His word and apply it in our lives. Yes, you have helped me to find His truth and apply it to my life. Now I get to watch each of you do the same. Thanks for sharing your lives with me. And we will always be grateful for your mother and my first wife, Francine. She blessed me with the two of you! Francine instilled in each of you a loving and grateful heart. God blessed us with her, and she is now in heaven with Jesus!

In my professional and educational life I was introduced to Stephen Covey's " Seven Habits of Highly Effective People", and I have applied that in this book. Thanks, Stephen, for your enlightenment.

In my times of reflections, I was guided to Don Bartlette. Don had a very, very hard and challenging life. His life's story led me to him singing "I Will Never Walk Alone".I wanted others to know his story and hopefully, hear him sing this song. Thanks, Don, for sharing and living for Christ.

Karen and Adam shared their love for God and their family with me in such a way that only God could orchestrate. They opened their hearts to Liz and me. Together we experienced the compassion of Jesus. Our Savior lives lovingly and softly in Karen and Adam's lives!Their love for Christ and their family is so great.I will be forever grateful that I was a part of witnessing His Amazing Grace at work. Thank you,Adam and Karen.

As for our Veterans, I would like to thank my brothers and sisters who served this great nation with a courage and a love of country that continued and will continue until they meet our Lord. Without you, I would not have been able to write this book or worship freely the God of Peace, Mercy, and Joy!I would especially like to thank Joe, a veteran who is a compassionately truthful man of God. As a preacher, I found Joe to be a strong- minded and Bible-versed man. He did not hesitate to be compassionately truthful when questioned about our Lord and His word. Joe lives the life of a God-revering man. His attitude of serving is a tribute to all. Joe helped bring me closer to God, and he did this through his love for our Father. Thanks, Joe, to both you and your lovely and beautiful wife Cindy.

Two people, Evan and Sue, have been inspirational and dear friends for many years, and I mean many! In fact, Evan performed at our wedding (Liz and I).Sue and Liz became close soon after our wedding several years ago and have enjoyed each others' friendship. Evan, on the other hand, is a friend who actually knows how to push my buttons; and he is very good at it (just kidding). Evan has been there for me throughout the years. His outlook on life is driven by his compassionate truthfulness. Evan has always been truthful, whether to me or his family or whomever! He will be straight with you; and you might not like what he is saying, but it will be true. This is one of the qualities lacking in our culture today, and that is the reason I appreciate Evan's friendship. God bless you, Evan.

Thank you, Paula, for taking some of your precious time to edit this writing. Please stay well and allow others to help you, as you helped me.

To all of the above: May God's Blessings, Grace, Peace, Mercy, Joy, and Love be upon each and every one of you!

Table of Contents

Chapter 1..1
The Journey Begins

Chapter 2..5
Tailgating Is Dangerous

Chapter 3..9
Fear, because I Can

Chapter 4.. 13
Responsibility & Accountability

Chapter 5.. 15
Surrendering through compassionate truthfulness

Chapter 6.. 17
Stay of Sound Mind

Chapter 7..21
Finding Courage to Change

Chapter 8.. 25
Today

Chapter 9.. 29
Listening v Hearing

Chapter 10...31
Spirituality

Chapter 11 33
You within the daily challenges

CHAPTER 12 37
Together with Him

CHAPTER 13 41
Seeking v Running

CHAPTER 14 43
He Will Strengthen Me

CHAPTER 15 47
You and Those Who are There for You

CHAPTER 16 49
Should I change my name to Job?

CHAPTER 17 53
Servitude Attitude: Healing begins with Serving

CHAPTER 18 57
Starting the Journey Home

CHAPTER 19 61
Love does not behave rudely, does not seek its own, is not provoked, thinks no evil, does not rejoice in iniquity but rejoices in TRUTH!

CHAPTER 20. 65
Softly and Gently Sharing God

FINAL CHAPTER 71
Compassionate Truthfulness is possible when a person is truthful and trustworthy to others and themselves

A LIGHT HAS COME ON. 75

Chapter 1
THE JOURNEY BEGINS

As we begin this journey together, I am reminded of all the love I have experienced during my time on this earth. I have loved and been loved by so many honest, lovely, and virtuous people that I am almost overwhelmed by their unconditional love and resolve.

So let us begin the journey by determining the essential qualities that define us as humans. We have so much input in our lives allowing us to think how we want to be, how we want to care for others, and, most of all, ourselves. So let's begin with the words that can determine our world through our choices:

Victim, survivor, powerless, revenge, anxiety, fear (the big one), disobedience, abandonment, hate (another big one) are the choices we make that allow our world to be negative. Always looking for the tailgaters, always finding a reason to doubt, and always finding a reason to be angry, which in turn allows us to seek revenge!

Honesty, truth, love (the biggest one), caring, courage, hope, and sound mind are the choices we make to allow our world to be positive. A world of continuing light, of warmth, tears of joy, and always being thankful!

So let us take some time to visit with a man, Mick, who suffered violent abuse as a child and as a teenager. Mick only let those dearest to him know what had taken place in his life when he was a young child and teenager. Jerome, Mick's stepfather, threw the frightened ten-year-old onto the couch. Mick winced from the impact, as his chest struck the wooden frame that ran across the front edge of the seat. It was padded, but the padding was so thin that it afforded little protection. Then Jerome grabbed his ear and twisted it. He applied such force that Mick thought Jerome was going to tear his ear off. The pain was consuming him, leading to Mick crying and begging Jerome not to hurt him again. The more he begged, the more Jerome seemed to enjoy this sadistic game twisting Mick's ear even harder. Jerome was extremely abusive to Mick and Mick's mother, Emma. Jerome was 6'2" tall and had an athletic build. Therefore, we can conclude that Mick was a victim of severe physical abuse; and as we visit with Mick we will verify the physical abuse he experienced, during his life, as a child.

Mick was powerless. "For God's sake Jerome! No!" Emma screamed. A few seconds later Jerome is dragging Emma by her hair. Mick noticed blood on her blouse and saw that her nose was bleeding. As he stared at her in shock and disbelief he realized she looked different. It took a few seconds before he saw her nose was lying on her left cheek and that blood was running from her nose into her mouth and a mixture of saliva and blood ran down her neck. Jerome was beating Emma because Jerome was drunk, not only from alcohol, but with his immense anger towards Mick. Jerome continued to beat Emma and scream at Mick. Mick sat and watched as his mother was battered. He wanted to help, but he was too afraid. He didn't want to be hurt again. All the while he hated himself for his fear. All he could do was sit and weep. Mick was powerless, and his life could have ended as a victim of violent physical abuse! Could one survive this abuse?

So let's take a look at what defines a survivor: a person who continues to function or prosper in spite of opposition, hardship, or setbacks. Can a Vietnam veteran, Joseph, be a survivor? Could Joseph be seen as a survivor? A man who experienced severe trauma while serving in the U.S. Army, due to being physically wounded and suffering extreme hostility from the enemy. What does a survivor do to continue functioning in the world after being discharged from the service? Is Joseph able to dispel all this personal trauma and prosper in his life's quest?

So we must visit the "survivor" definition again to truly find how a person does survive!

Maybe Joseph will seek revenge throughout his life by seeking methods of self-destruction: self-inflicting wounds, suicide, reliving traumatic events over and over, drug/alcohol abuse, and physical abuse to his family members. We will continue defining "survivor" through the next few paragraphs.

Does a survivor experience anxiety—the intense, excessive, and persistent worry and fear about everyday situations? Does this include stress? Stress plays a huge role in how Joseph finds his way through his anxiety. The stress is not from an overwhelming incident; rather, it is what we stated above, it was from the everyday situations he faced in Vietnam.

Next we have 15-year-old Josie, a foster child who has been involved with drugs, alcohol, and self-inflicting wounds. Josie believes she has to have "pain" for her life to be normal. As severe anxiety and/or stress become overwhelming to her, she begins the self-destructive behaviors. Usually, Josie will start with cutting her arms or legs. This began several years ago, and now it is hard to find a place on her body without a scar. Josie finds peace in drugs because they prevent her from focusing on her pain, her blame pain! Josie started this because her mother was abusive to her, physically, emotionally, and mentally; thus, all treatment centered on her abuse. Josie never allowed adults to get close. All adult directives were defied because Josie knew this would anger them. She refused to accept any affection or care. This would only cause more pain because after the care/love came the abuse, neglect and more pain! Is Josie a victim? Of course she is! Is Joseph a victim? Of course he is! Is Josie a survivor? Her journey is ongoing, and only time will tell; plus, she will need the right kind of help. Is Joseph a survivor? Yes, he is; and his PTSD still exists but only in memory, not in his physical and emotional life. Joseph found healing through a compassionately truthful being—Jesus!

There is a time for everything, and a season for every activity under the heavens: a time to be born and a time to die, a time to plant and a time to uproot, a time to kill and a time to heal, a time to tear down and a time to build, a time to weep and a time to dance, a time to scatter stones and a time to gather them, a time to embrace and a time to refrain from embracing, a time to search and a time to give up, a time to keep and a time to throw away, a time to tear and a time to mend, a time to be silent and a time to speak, a time to love and a time to hate, a time for war and a time for peace. (Ecclesiastes 3:1-8)

Chapter 2

TAILGATING IS DANGEROUS

EARLY IN CHAPTER ONE WE MENTIONED: AS WE keep our eyes on the tailgaters, we find reasons to doubt, reasons to be angry, reasons to be anxious, and reasons to fear! We do this by always looking at what we did in the past or what we accept "happened to us"! We seek to hear what others will tell us: what went wrong and how we were so mistreated. All this does is make the pain worse, allowing us to blame our past for present behaviors. That is how we keep the pain alive—looking for our tailgaters!

As a survivor, what can I do? I am the victim, and no one can change it. Got it? No one! Unable to escape our past, we run from it, hope that it will go away or find something that will make it go away—further abuse or drugs or alcohol! We push and push, without thought, just hurrying to move the pain out of our way! Is that not what we do when we tailgate? We make people move out of our way.

Not all people get out of the way when we tailgate. A young man experienced this as he was driving on a Sunday afternoon to a flag football game. As usual, he was running late and was in a huge hurry. He was on a two-lane road and was speeding. Soon there was a nice new pick-up truck in front of him that was not going fast enough so he began to tailgate. The small distance between the two vehicles definitely displeased the truck driver. It was not long before the he stopped his truck in front of the young man's vehicle, got out, and walked back to the young man's vehicle. The young man rolled down his window to ask if something was wrong. Immediately, the truck driver punched the young man in the nose, then returned to his truck and left. The young man then drove to the game, bloody nose and all. Upon arrival, his friends were concerned about his well-being because there was blood on his car door and his shirt. He began to explain what happened, and his friends responded with: "When are you going to figure it out? Tailgating is only going to cause you or someone else pain!"

    Staying in the past is not going to make anyone better, and tailgating demonstrates that! Focusing on the wrongs of our past, what we did or was done to us is very dangerous! Just like the young man who had his nose bloodied found out. You push and push the cars in front of you, and most move off to the side. However, when you push with your pain/anger while driving, problems, big problems, can occur—accidents, possibly fatal accidents, children hurt, and vehicles ruined. And we caused this accident; we are accountable for the consequences we receive—paying for the deductible on the vehicle damage! Criminal charges can apply also—vehicle manslaughter! Yet tailgating goes on until the unforgettable and unforgivable happens. We push, and we push, knowing this is wrong! I am in charge, and I will do what I want when I want! It's my pain; it's my hurt; and someone else caused it. Therefore, I will take what is mine; I hurt others because I hurt; and they hurt me! Got it? Then deal with it!

    Come on, get out of my way! Can't you see I need you to move out of my way? Then, boom, as we travel over the top of the hill, boom! There was a traffic jam; and we are speeding, way too fast and could not stop! If that traffic jam had not been there nothing would have happened! Can't you see, I have to push it because if I don't, it will catch up to me! And it's not my fault! If you had been treated like I have then you would understand. Nope, you can't and never will understand; no one will! So, get out of my way and if there is another traffic jam, oh well, then I have another and another and another...

We can state the following: If you want to get some place on time leave on time or early. If you find yourself in a pinch and do need to get somewhere quickly, tailgating only angers others or causes accidents. A solution could be to let people know it is an emergency by flashing your lights. Most people will pull off to the side. It's the same way with our past, and we will look at ways to have people pull over for us in later chapters.

Take my yoke upon you and learn from me, for I am gentle and humble in heart, and you will find rest for your souls. For my yoke is easy and my burden is light. (Matt 11:28-30)

Chapter 3

Fear, because I can

Johnny, just 14 years old, was walking home through the park for the first time alone. Johnny always made sure someone was with him; but on this day, he could not find a companion. Usually, he would be talking to someone or listening to them, but not today. His mind went back to when his mother would be angry and start yelling at his dad. His dad would leave for the bar down the street. Later, Mom would send Johnny to get his dad to prevent dad from falling and ending up in a ditch somewhere. As usual, dad was drunk and very hard to manage! Going into this rough old bar was not something Johnny liked—nor was the dark walk through some alleys. Getting dad home was a task. Johnny had to get past other drunk and cruel people in the bar. Johnny's dad never wanted to leave, and the walk home was worse. Dad would be drunk and physical, giving Johnny many hard whacks and punches. Then the other drunks would be mean too! So, yeah, Johnny was thinking this as he began his walk. The anxiety was overwhelming; and Johnny just started to run and run, his stress level high and increasing. Would these thoughts ever go away? No, because as he walked into his house with his Dad the fighting began . The anxiety and stress went up a few more notches. Along with the fighting there was blaming going on that included Johnny! He was accused of not doing his share around the house. Johnny was not working and not bringing any money into the family! How could he expect to be fed if did not bring in some money? So the fighting turned on Johnny! More anxiety and more stress, which meant Johnny was closing in on an outburst. He was about to show them his rage! Yes, knock some crap out of this family! Yet he found he was no match for his dad, and his dad seemed to enjoy kicking his butt! Now this added to his fears, anxiety, and stress! So Johnny began the slippery slope down to the "fear of never being good enough". Johnny began seeking other ways to make his fear go away. Alcohol, drugs, and other self-destructive behaviors became a norm. Johnny kept an eye on his rear-view mirror. His past kept him in the life-style that he was in—the road to his self-destruction.

He had tailgaters, and he tailgated; so there was always a push, a very hard push to get out of the way or get knocked out of the way! Johnny's life was in a very fast and hard downward spiral! "Get out of my way! My life hurts, so get out of my way! If you don't like it, get over it, and get out of my way! Man, life is cruel; and I hurt; so stay out of my life! No, no, I do not want your words, your stupid words. There is no love there, and I am totally free of any love. How could anyone expect me to think any different after all I've been through! Get out of my way and stay away!" Yeah, there is no hope here.

Johnny is now defeated and wants only to deal with his pain the way he wants—flame the blame and seek revenge and vengeful disobedience.

Lois, Johnny's mom, is fine the way her house is—in total chaos. This is how she has lived her life, and Lois is the best at blaming everyone and anyone for her problems. And do not dare to call her out on it because Lois has the answer: "It is not my fault! I am not healthy because of my husband or Johnny. I am this way because my sister did this or my neighbor did that." The list goes on and on.

Lois fears reality and copes with her fear by blaming others, which allows her to not deal with any of her fears! Lois fears because she can.

Chuck, Johnny's dad, knew Lois's issues prior to marrying her. It didn't matter to him since he could drink his way through anything, even his mom abandoning him as a 6-year-old. Chuck's mom left without telling him good-bye. His mom was never heard from again. He never tried to find her because his dad was always angry about her leaving and blamed him for it. So Chuck was okay with being blamed for something. Chuck felt if Lois stopped blaming him then something else was wrong. Chuck began drowning his fears with alcohol when he was 15 years old. He has never stopped drinking and is now 44 years old. Oops, he did try to quit once; but about 4 days of sobriety was all he could handle. Other fears started to appear—Johnny's downward spiral, Lois' problems with her past, work, etc...

Looking for fear and finding it is easy. Dealing with your fear is also easy. What's hard is giving up your fears. Without these fears our lives change dramatically. The question becomes can I handle my fears? The better question is: Do I want to deal with my fears because I want to be accountable for my actions and learn to respond differently when processing my thoughts?

Do everything without grumbling or arguing, so that you may become blameless and pure, children of God... (Philippians 2:14-15)

Chapter 4

Responsibility: The Ability to Respond
Accountability: The Ability to Accept Your Outcome

DAN AND BOB WANT TO GO ON A VACATION NEXT March, somewhere warm! They agree to save the $1,800.00 (each) over the next 14 months (preferably 12). They figure at least $150.00 per month will do it. The savings begin in January. Bob is doing great. He puts $200.00 away because after the basketball games on Saturdays he goes straight home instead of down to the pizza shop with all the guys, which also saves on beer costs, a lot of beer. Dan goes along with the guys each Saturday; thus, the money is not being saved. This continues through March; then softball season starts in May and Bob has over $600.00 saved while Dan only has $150.00. Softball season is even harder—especially for Dan. However, Bob is determined, and the next 4 months nets another $600.00. Dan, not concerned about saving the required amount, simply assumes neither of them will go on vacation should he come up short. This means Bob would have the $1800.00 as extra money for them to spend. At the end of 12 months Bob has the $1,800.00 and is headed to Cancun, Mexico for 10 days, and Dan can't believe Bob is going without him. Accountability goes both ways: if you did it, you get it, and if you did not, then you get 0! Plain and simple. However, Dan did not get it, and did not accept it. Either Bob takes him on vacation, or together they stay home; and Dan helps Bob spend the $1800 he saved. Does Dan have the ability to respond? Of course not, and will not accept being accountable for not following through with his commitment—saving money for his vacation.

A man at the age of 62 feels he has been pushed aside; his employment is gone. "How dare anyone push me around! I am a proud man; and from now on whoever gets in my way, I will take care of them." It's around noon on a workday and this man, Sonny, has been drinking. He is driving back to his little farm and sees two teenage boys unloading brush from a pick-up truck onto someone's property. Now this makes him mad, and he slams on the brakes! I'm going to tear into these two punks and teach them who is boss in this part of the country, he thinks! He pulls his truck right behind the boys' truck and jumps out of his truck. He screams while charging the teenagers, "What the f___ do you think you are doing? Who said you could do this?" Sonny goes back to his truck and puts his 44 magnum pistol into his right hand. He yells while waving his pistol, "Do you f____g think I'm going to let this to happen? Do you think I'm f_____g kidding?" Is Sonny acting like a person who is able to respond accordingly? Sonny knows that when he drinks early in the day he gets angry, and it only takes a few drinks to get very angry. Yet, he feels no wrong has been done here, even though he knows it is something that better never happen to his family. Remember responsibility is defined by having the ability to respond. Sadly, Sonny has never learned this ability; he just uses his fears to arm himself with the ability to get mad.

Sonny and Dan both cannot accept what has happened to them. Sonny won't admit that his employment ended due to his failure to bring his company to a higher level of sales. His way of thinking was the right way and showboating was his way, very full of himself. Whereas Dan just liked to have fun and did not see any connection between not saving the money and not going on vacation. The vacation was just a foolish idea. Neither man can see the trees because of the forest!

For God did not give us a spirit of timidity, but a spirit of power, of love, and of self-discipline. (2 Timothy 1:7)

Chapter 5
SURRENDERING THROUGH COMPASSIONATE TRUTHFULNESS

OUR EARTHLY JOURNEY BEGINS TO FIND JOY, peace, love, hope and mercy when we commit to God. However it's not the person who is striving for healing; rather it is those around him or her, as they start the journey together. It could be some of the parents, siblings, and friends who believe they are not the ones with all of the problems. They see the wrongs committed by others and pass judgment on them. They strive for attention by making blaming statements: "My son needs to change his ways. Or my sister cannot see what she is doing is so bad, and when I point it out she gets worse!" On and on they go; however, what does Christ want us to do? What would He want the son or sister to do? Christ is truthful, compassionately truthful and honest; and He states in Matthew 19:26 "With God all things are possible." When we are living for Christ, we strive to be Christ-like; gratefully, we endeavor to be compassionately truthful.

Mick and I were discussing this loving approach, and you will love how Mick explained it to me. Well, you decide on Mick's version of compassionately truthful: Tell the person you are with the truth, even if it concerns the person's appearance. Mick goes on by telling me about the mirror experiment: Tell a person to close his or her eyes; then walk them in front of a mirror and say: "Open your eyes when I count to 3!" Mick counts to 3, and the person jumps back upon opening her eyes. "See, you scared yourself! I told you you were ugly!" I know that was said in jest; however, if someone is doing something wrong and we know it is wrong, then it is wrong. Now, that person knows it is wrong; yet we say "Aww, you'll be okay; just hang in there." Or we say, "Look in the mirror and scare yourself." Neither response is what Christ would do. Let the person know you care through the love of Christ, and you will be there for them, to support them in a compassionate and truthful manner. Be Christ-like—compassionate and truthful.

This is especially critical when you are trying to help someone with alcoholism or addiction. Telling them to hang in there because it will be better tomorrow will not and has not worked, ever! Be compassionately truthful and get them the help they need now! A lot of people believe the alcoholics or addicts have to reach bottom, or they have to want to do it! Then we wait, wait, and wait until they are in trouble criminally or have hurt someone else (e.g., car wreck, etc...) or themselves to the point of no return. God put someone into the lives of those who made it to make sure they received the help they needed. These compassionate and truthful people did not accept the "maybe later and wait concept". They were compassionately honest and had them get the help they needed.

Here's an example: What is the reason a veteran will accept help from another veteran? Because a veteran will have compassion and will be honest. This is what a brotherhood is all about—being truthful and honest through the love of Christ. A young man has been traumatized by what he went through in combat. We could tell him that in time it will be better; meanwhile, he needs help now! He has been seeking help and wants to find it. Whether the choice he makes is the right one will be determined by our wanting to let him find his own way or by being compassionately truthful. Too many veterans commit suicide daily, somewhere around 20 + per day. Yet we wait and are not compassionately truthful with them, and they know it. They feel alone and defeated. However, it does not need to be that way when we serve our brothers by being compassionately truthful, as Christ always is and will be!

Let all you do be done in love. (1 Corinthians 16:14)

Chapter 6
STAY OF SOUND MIND

AS WE CONTINUE OUR JOURNEY TOGETHER LET'S be of sound mind and hope! Let's share His joy and peace through our compassionate honesty! Does an eight-year-old girl know how to find joy and peace when all she knows is verbal and physical abuse? The significant adult has not expressed any love, any belonging. So we go in with the mirror complex: she needs to accept the truth; we will be brash and this child will have to deal with it! Back up the truck! That is what this child has experienced— verbal and physical abuse. Thus, all we get is continuing hurtful and painful behaviors to themselves and others. It hurts the caretakers to watch this happen over and over. This will not change until we are completely compassionate and thoroughly honest with not only the child but with God! God loves us so much that he gave His only Son for us; and He never gave up on us, then, now, and forever. This child is asking for this type of love; but everywhere she has turned has been nothing but turmoil, anything but love and hope! Then we want to put this child in a residential treatment facility where she will have to change. She has been there and done that! The response will be the same—more and more of the hurt and pain!It sounds like we are continually beating a drum over and over because we keep saying the same thing! We'll continue to treat this child in this manner: "We know what is right so let's put a helmet on her head. This will protect her head while she beats it against a wall until her head bleeds. Then up her medication until she can barely function!" I ask: "Is this a compassionate way to help a child overcome her brutal beginnings? Are the treatment/service personnel of sound mind or of a worldly mind?"

Here's another example: there is the little 8 year-old-boy who cannot, seriously, walk and chew gum at the same time due to the severe beatings he received in his earlier years. This child, Jimmy, goes to school every day at the residential setting where he was placed 8 months ago. Jimmy's daily after-school schedule requires him to join in a group with the other 10 children about his age to do a craft. However he cannot do crafts because of his physical disabilities. His eyes and hands do not work together. Because he will act out and have to be restrained if forced to attend this group, Jimmy is allowed to watch ESPN. Yet, everyday the staff, after the group is done with crafts, confronts Jimmy because he did not attend the group activity. They take the TV remote from him and put him in a timeout!

Let's take a deeper look at what Jimmy is experiencing: he would love to play baseball, basketball, football, soccer, and other sports but cannot because of his brain damage. Having developed a passion to watch sports, he behaves in school all day so he can watch sports. Again, staff proved they were not of sound mind because they used this passion as a way to get Jimmy to participate in school, then would take away his passion to get what they wanted—to show Jimmy he must do what he is directed to do. Thus, Jimmy would act out and the staff would restrain him, 2 or 3 times each and every afternoon. Because Jimmy was always being restrained he did not qualify for a step-down unit or foster care. The more restraints Jimmy had, the longer the wait. However, due to a compassionate and truthful administrator, staff was directed to find out what Jimmy wanted—find his passion! Soon, Jimmy would watch sports and then listen to his new radio. Jimmy was so excited and began to smile each and every day. His restraints ended the day he received the new very durable construction radio. Jimmy proved to be very durable as well. Although he experience all these adult messes, he was still able to begin trusting adults, which ended the restraints. In 2 months, Jimmy was in a step-down unit and ready to begin foster care!

A sound mind will make compassionate and truthful decisions based on Jesus' compassionate and truthful love. As Joseph, our veteran friend stated; "The trauma I have faced in my early life does not disappear. It is still there and real. However, I now know the triggers, and I do not allow the negative thoughts and hurts back into my life. Joseph has developed a sound mind. How did he do this, and will the above -mentioned little girl and boy be able to develop a sound mind, along with a spirit of hope and unconditional love? Joseph found God through his wife because she was of sound mind, a child of God who has unconditional love. So, yes, the two children will do the same if they continue to find adults with a sound mind who see them as a gift from God.

An anxious heart weighs a man down, but a kind word cheers him up. (Proverbs 12:25)

restraints. In 2 months, Jimmy was in a step-down unit and ready to begin foster care!

A sound mind will make compassionate and truthful decisions based on Jesus' compassionate and truthful love. As Joseph, our veteran friend stated; "The trauma I have faced in my early life does not disappear. It is still there and real. However, I now know the triggers, and I do not allow the negative thoughts and hurts back into my life. Joseph has developed a sound mind. How did he do this, and will the above -mentioned little girl and boy be able to develop a sound mind, along with a spirit of hope and unconditional love? Joseph found God through his wife because she was of sound mind, a child of God who has unconditional love. So, yes, the two children will do the same if they continue to find adults with a sound mind who see them as a gift from God.

An anxious heart weighs a man down, but a kind word cheers him up. (Proverbs 12:25)

Chapter 7

FINDING COURAGE TO CHANGE

CAN YOU IMAGINE HOW IT WOULD BE TO LIVE IN a foreign country and not be able to understand the language? On top of this, most of the time the weather was much colder than your homeland. Imagine a life of abuse from all the adults in your life making the only connection to an adult in your past very disturbing. When all the adults associated with your life seemed untrustworthy, how could you understand what love or belonging means or how it feels? It's just been emotional, spiritual and physical pain. How can one communicate within a world like this and exist or want to exist?

Living in this new world will be very difficult. These new adults want to call it your new home. How could you call it home when you do not know what a home is or even feels like? Then this new family says they want to love you and provide a happy home. Love, what is love? How do you find happiness? Even better, what is joy? Someone needs to explain so you can understand, but in your language, not this language that you barely understand.

No one is communicating in a manner you understand, and getting very mad is the choice you make. You demand to be left alone! Again, this didn't work because no one was listening! So you show them how mad you can get! So you put 3 new holes in the wall; and you will continue to do it over and over, until you are left alone! You hate this place! They do not have any idea what your hurt is and how much pain you are experiencing today. Again you demand to be left alone.

Now they want to fix you with therapeutic treatment methods, which continuously state the same thing: We understand how difficult it must be in this new environment. Really, same old same old! They believe you are demonizing this new home and wrecking their house while still calling this place your new home, whatever that is. Of course they think you need some big time medication to control your behaviors so it's off to see a psychiatrist who will prescribe medication. After taking it for a little while you continue to wreck their house because your pain and hurt have not diminished. In other words, you have become worse! All the kids you ran with in your home country (at the orphanage) understood you because they had the same hurt and pain you did. You destroyed other things together to cause the other kids and adults to feel your pain. It sure was more fun there! You had figured out how to get what you wanted when you wanted, it no matter what! Now they want you to conform to their world, their rules, because they think they understand you. If they understood you then they would leave you alone. They do not because they do not understand your previous life: how your past continues to affect your behaviors and emotions.

Hey, what's this new stuff they are showing you? This garbage called "unconditional love"? Is it any different from what they have tried to push you into believing? They know you will not let go of your past, and yet they focus on this forgiveness crap. Forgiveness, oh yeah, they forgive you when you screw up, yet you continue to mess with them because it shows them what it is like to be betrayed and left alone. They will feel a little of your pain, your hurt. Then, maybe, they will let you be. They keep on tailgating by going back to your past, constantly believing it will completely take over your life! Wait, what is that? They actually believe that you can trust them, maybe, because they want you to start trusting yourself? Huh? How does that work? You are starting to understand what's going on here. Your past is not you; you do not have to let it define you. Yes, up until now you have let you past define you! Now you can begin to move on and take charge of your life. These changes start today— not yesterday and not tomorrow. Oh my gosh, you are not sure how this works; yet, you know what did not work—living your life through a rear view mirror and focusing on the tailgating.

You realize you weren't loved, especially during your first 3 years on earth.

Understanding this new way of approaching life is difficult because it does not make your past go way; it just changes how you live each day. Yet you wonder how to apply this in your life and to make each new day better. So this change begins by changing your behaviors for the next hour.

A young child finds belonging to an adoptive family very difficult. Setting a very rigorous and strict schedule adds to the difficulties each child is up against each and every day. How would you feel if you woke up every day facing a terminal disease because you unknowingly did something very wrong? Therefore, you would not be aware of any repercussions.Does this compare to what this child is experiencing? We understand what someone could be going through when they are diagnosed with a terminal disease, but we do not understand what a child or adult is going through after experiencing trauma or a lack of love in early life. No hugs, no sweet kisses on the cheek from a loving mother, no bouncing on a daddy's knee. So all they know is pain, especially when all they received was continuous badgering and abuse, each and every day, all day long. Can one imagine never experiencing unconditional love? Let's take the time to listen, to understand each child's pain and allow each child to find and understand forgiveness! Help the child be thankful for today! Let the child experience compassionate truthfulness, and allow the child to let go of the tailgaters so the child can live in the here and now.

Permit these children to finally experience love that can be found in a family, a loving touch of a mother when her child scrapes a knee, the reassuring hug and smile from a father when a child has a nightmare. These adoptive parents are gifts from God who never expected to have sleepless nights because of their new child's nightmares or attempts of self-harm.

These parents are feeling betrayed or mislead and all alone! Some even reach the point of wanting to rethink or even cancel the adoption. Prayer and a church full of people helping them through this stressful time is the answer.

Unconditional love is for all of us, not just for the adoptive parents. We can and will make a difference when we act through the wisdom God has let us acquire! He is all loving and will never give up on us! So we begin with our church reaching out with commitment to be there when these parents need a shoulder to lean on or someone to listen to their questions. Listening helps; being negative by going along with their complaining only keeps their emotional pain alive! It's hard in the beginning, yet each day brings the child closer to understanding forgiveness. Focus on today; never look into the rear-view mirror. God told us to forgive those who have caused us pain. It is hard for us to do that, and now we expect this child who does not understand forgiveness to forgive! This is where unconditional love is applied.

The greatest example is Jesus Christ. As he was experiencing torture and physical pain on the cross, He cried out: "Forgive them, Father, for they know not what they do!"(Luke 23:34) Jesus is our Savior who was and is totally compassionate and always truthful. He gave us a way to forgive ourselves and others. Let's pass this on to those who do not know how to forgive or love unconditionally by not judging others. When you know love and have experienced it through Him you will have a joy and peace that allows you to share this with others. Run the race; never give up on forgiveness. Use your confidence in God to shine bright when you walk into a home that cries out for love. Your wisdom will guide you when you ask God to be with you in this time of challenges. He will bless you, and the answers will come. Confidence in God and prayer will guide you and will soon be noticed by those you are serving.

Judge not, and you will not be judged; condemn not, and you will not be condemned; forgive and you will be forgiven. (Luke 6:37)

Chapter 8
TODAY

BEING THANKFUL FOR TODAY! POWERFUL words, very powerful words, and yes, you can do it. You are on this earth for a purpose, and loving your neighbor is part of that purpose. If you let them suffer and do not reach out with compassionate truth and honesty, then how can you get through your today?

Therefore, let's begin with the word "trust". First you must trust the Lord and trust yourself; then you can trust others. You must be sincere about commitment because the people who challenge trust from others do not trust themselves! Hence, when a person begins to trust, others are able to enter their lives. This takes time and commitment, along with acceptance, sincere acceptance. Words are spoken, and trust is broken. Therefore, once committed you must be ready and able for their trust and mistrust.

You could cause harm to someone who has experienced severe trauma if you are not compassionate. This traumatized person does not need doubters and mistrust. No, they need Compassionately Truthful people in their lives. They suffered enough to recognize more lies, and prescribed medication will not be the answer to their horror. To them life sucks, plain and simple: life sucks!!!! Here are a child's thoughts: all you want me to do is listen to you talk and talk and talk some more. Nope, that is not going to happen. The pain will not be talked away; nor will it be medicated away. Each individual will seek the truth through any means possible to put an end to their pain, sadness, loneliness, and nightmares.

Today can be the day a person starts to hear and feel the truth, compassionate truth! Easier said then done though because the doubts could begin to creep back into their lives! How can one move on from the ugliness that keeps taking and taking? This person will call each and every false word out; in fact, it becomes a way of life. So what do you do when faced with this wall of weariness? How do you get over it? Can you get around this person's wall of disbelief? Can we dig under the wall of pain and nightmares?

First you must get past your doubts—Over? Under? Around? This is not working, so start guiding this person with honorable and truthful interactions. Become a teacher of togetherness and forgiveness; therefore, it is time to share this without any promises or whims. A passion for giving is one of the keys to breaking down an emotional wall. Also, making it very clear that only truth will be presented by you and only truth will be accepted by you. No "ifs", "ands", or "buts" will be accepted.

A traumatized young man, Charlie, walks into an office seeking emotional and mental help. Soon the young man and the therapist reach the point where Charlie and the therapist share his pain. The therapist knows not to say, "I understand what you are going through" or "This has to be so hard and really painful." Soon Charlie hears, "I think you need some medicine to help you relax and numb the pain. How's that sound to you?" The therapist is a believer of "medication fixes everything". Charlie goes with it and wants the medication to work. Then the therapist asks his family how he is doing; and the answer is, "Not too good, he is on this medication that has him sleeping a lot. Then when he wakes up, he is usually in a dark mood; all he wants is to be left alone so he can relax. Then he takes more medication and etc., etc..."

Is this just another wall? Is Charlie's pain starting to decrease? Nope, not at all. Could Charlie respond to a dose of Compassionate Truthfulness? Let's give it a try.

Again, Charlie is going into an office to find a way through his wall of pain and suffering.

As Charlie begins to work with his therapist, he is reminded several times that honesty and care will be the focus of all meetings with Charlie. Charlie is not sure he wants to face this wall head-on. The pain might be unbearable; and all Charlie ever heard was to avoid the pain; just avoid it!So his fear the unbearable fear = 2X the fear which, understandingly, he is trying to avoid. Which means he is going to get worse.

Let's go back to his visit. As he moves through his first session he finds the therapist to be truly listening by asking for clarification several times concerning what Charlie said versus the therapist stating what it meant. Clearly advice is all Charlie had been given. He was now being asked for his view or his thoughts. Also,when he asked the therapist her interpretation Charlie would hear, "being truthful, let's keep moving forward so you can find your way to begin the healing." Later he would hear, "Being honest, it seems this is still a huge barrier to you; what do you think?" Charlie is now engaged in learning how to face the truth with his therapist's compassionate yet truthful guidance. It is hard, very hard to face the truth when the truth is going to hurt! In fact, it is something worth avoiding. Just ask Charlie—No gain, no pain. We just leave it to keep getting deeper and deeper until we just cannot take it any more. Then it is usually too late. Damage has been done: threats, running away, pushing people away, and blaming God for everything.

Being compassionately truthful will move Charlie further away from his trauma and closer to moving forward with his life. Yes, Charlie can and will do this through real truth—Godly truth! Listening to Charlie, really listening and helping him knock down each wall will bring him closer to healing and closer to God, a new beginning! He began today with the sun in his face, listening to the birds sing.

Finally, all of you have unity of spirit, sympathy, love of the brethren, a tender heart and a humble mind. (1 Peter 3:8)

Chapter 9
LISTENING V HEARING

THIS WILL BE A SHORT CHAPTER DUE TO THE common sense of listening instead of hearing. You have 2 ears and 1 mouth. As a listener, it just makes sense that you should do twice as much listening than talking. If we are going to help the Charlies of the world then let's start by listening. In becoming a very good listener, you learn the following: Only when you truly listen to what the person is saying will you be able to stop just hearing the words; then you can respond to his needs. Wow, you are great! How can you be compassionately truthful when you are not listening to what the Charlies are opening their hearts about? So the question is not what answers do we have; rather, are we compassionately truthful listeners?

Next, you look at the hearing only mode: totally focused on today and hopefully, you can tune in to Charlie when needed. Did you pay the gas bill? What are you doing tonight? Did you get paid this week? So on and so on. If you are listening to your thoughts when with Charlie and others, are they going to trust you? And they will know! So just hearing does not and will not work!

While attending a company meeting, you observe two of your colleagues: one, who is not paying attention to the speaker and one who is listening very intensely, even taking notes, as the speaker is making some statements that are very critical to company work assignments. Now you are asked to partner-up with a person from this meeting. Would you choose the daydreamer or the intense listener? Of course you would choose the second person, the intense listener. This is where you can put it all together. Because you listened and by crossing all the t's and dotting all the i's with the listener you know where to go with this assignment. Is this what a traumatized person wants—to work with someone who listens? Or would you want to work with the other attendee and have to do all the work, probably missing some important steps that would have resulted in a much better outcome? The traumatized person knows this path well because they have been down this road again and again and again—a path most traveled! So let's proceed to a road less traveled!

Greater love has no one than this, that he lay down his life for his friends. (John 15:13)

Chapter 10
Spirituality

AH, YES, THE ROAD LESS TRAVELED, THE INFAmous **Y** in the road that challenges each and every one of us! As you approach this **Y**, you begin to think about making the choice based on what is right for you. Then as you process these two choices, another thought comes into play—what is the right thing to do, period. No matter the outcome or how it affects me. God created us to make choices—free will. He also gave us the ability to learn right from wrong. As life goes on, we begin to distort the ways that lead us into making the right choice. Hence, we can take the wrong road. A wise and spiritually healthy person seeks the truth, a road of forgiveness and love. This is not to be interpreted as being weak or unable to complete the journey. It takes a very courageous person to seek out joy and forgiveness in times of hurt and pain.

A spiritual person, a child of God, will look for wisdom and healing based on a faith of peace, joy, hope, and love. This person begins a race with thoughts of finishing it, while doing the best he can! Winning is great, but finishing is the best! While doing all you can, always finish it. A person's wholeness includes this person's spirituality. This is where God is, each and every day, He is there for us. No matter how we try to take the wrong road, God always shows up on the road we choose. What we do while on that road determines what we become. The wisdom comes from the right choices we have made; and, sometimes, we learn from the wrong choices we have made. Also, we learn from not making a decision until we process the **Y**, which includes praying to the Lord. He provides the peace in choosing the path we are to take, a joyful and peaceful road! A road that is not easy and is less taken!

Yet, when someone suffers a traumatic event, that person discovers the road is rocky, has many pot holes, and is very steep! This is where our spirituality comes into play. Are we looking for worldly happiness and peace? Spirituality is completely and compassionately committing to a way of life that includes our Lord, Jesus Christ, each and every day!

Do not be anxious about anything, but in everything by prayer and supplication with thanksgiving let your requests be made known to God. And the peace of God, which surpasses all understanding, will guard your hearts and your minds in Christ Jesus. (Philippians 4:6-7)

Chapter 11

You within the Daily Challenges

Let's go back to the forward of this book and take a look at the lyrics to the song "You'll Never Walk Alone". Storm, dark, wind, rain, and golden sky, silver song of a lark, all point to hope. Once you begin your life's journey there will be challenges. And yes, there will be hope; and many times, as we learn how to make decisions based on righteousness, hope turns into a blessing, even though you started the journey on the wrong foot. In other words, as the song goes, we will see the golden sky at the end of the storm. You can see this ending when you open your eyes and heart to the love of the Father. Doubters say, "Wow, is this a bunch of crap". Yet these same people jump right into taking any wonder drug that promises to make them better. Or better yet, they ask Google or Alexa for help! Who is listening to what? Our challenges will make us stronger, and we can move on with a Golden Sky when we open our eyes and heart to the wonders our God created. Many, many, people have lived through storms.

A young man, Paul, is in a college philosophy class. Paul is 23 years old, a confident and sharp young man. About halfway through the fall semester the topic of debate is pro-life versus anti-life. Paul sits in the middle of the classroom while Cindy, who is studying to become a nurse, sits alone in the last desk of the last row. Cindy is very sincere and tender as she shares her thoughts on this topic. Cindy talks for a little while then states; "Life should be protected unless the woman was raped." Paul quickly stated; "This is still murder." Cindy asks Paul to explain his reasoning. Paul did not respond. Then Cindy reiterated her opinion and again Paul stated; "It's still murder". Again Cindy kindly asked Paul to explain what he meant through his statement; again Paul remained quiet. This went back and forth two more times. Cindy was now frustrated and shouted: "Will you tell me what the f____ you mean? You are being a f____ g a____ e!" Then Paul responded to her outburst with the following: "My father was the rapist, and my mother was raped! If she took the road you are suggesting then I would not be here!" Paul knew what his mother went through; yet he chose to seek "the Golden Sky". He knew that she wanted to have joy and hope in her life that was driven by love. Paul's mother chose a road less traveled because she wanted the Golden Sky, and Paul knew his life got her through a very ugly and brutal storm. When he spoke of his mother, you could see the love he had for this beautiful and courageous woman! His mother's hope was much stronger than the storm; her love would halt any rain or winds. She never walked alone.

Challenges are there; we can try to sidestep them or deal with them. Sidestepping means we never move forward. Sooner or later they build up, and then maybe it is too late, or we now are in some deep and unforgiving quicksand. The key is we never walk alone, never! Our Father is always there. It is up to us to find the courage to seek Him and let Him walk with us, side by side. Some times He will even carry us. To be compassionately truthful, do not look in the rear-view mirror for answers. Seek wisdom through Him, and Him alone!

Many people have given everything they have, even their lives, just to be able to worship God; yet, we do not take the time to be thankful and count our blessings! What does this have to do with our daily challenges, a doubter asks? When one starts their day off with prayers of thanksgiving and joy is shared with others in one's life then a challenge will be taken in stride. No sidesteps needed! Life goes on, and so do we. We will be stronger. Paul's mother had to be strong during her pregnancy, and as she gave birth to Paul. And she grew stronger as she went through life with her beautiful son. So let's begin our walk with His Son.

But you, man of God, flee from all this, and pursue righteousness, godliness, faith, love, endurance and gentleness. (1 Timothy 6:11)

Chapter 12
TOGETHER WITH HIM

THIS QUESTION WAS FIRST ASKED MANY, MANY years ago: What walks on all fours early in life, then on two in the next phase and then on three late in life? How many times have you had to find answers to daily challenges that could or did make changes to your life? And possibly, life-changing decisions were needed immediately, which you had to make by yourself. How did it affect your family? Was there any pressure? How did this decision affect you and yours? Did others think you were wrong and become upset with you? Did you blame someone for making you choose the wrong way to complete a task?

What about blaming God for the trauma you faced? How could He take my wife or husband? If there is a God, how could He let my daughter be murdered by a drunk driver? The "hows" and "whys" syndrome—this is a road well traveled! We need someone to blame; and, if God is all about helping His children, then how or why did He let this tragic event happen to me?

Our lives are to be lived and there will be times when trauma occurs. It does hurt; and oh, how it weigh us down! We can relive it over and over until it overtakes us! How do I get past this? The "whys" and "hows" keep coming at us! The tailgaters are pushing us, over and over! We pull over and let them pass; however, soon another one shows up! We become weary and cannot keep this up! Then somebody states; "I understand what you are going through." That is when we lose it! "What, how can you be so-o-o-o stupid and say you understand what I am going through? Did you ever lose someone this young because of some idiots who were drag racing on the road in front of your house and one of the drivers lost control of his car and ran over your little boy right in front of your house, 500' from the road?" You become so angry, full of revenge! Nothing, and I mean nothing, can take this pain away!

The title of this chapter; "Together with Him", means having a strong faith in Jesus. Many of us believe we have this faith, and we are strong in our faith as long as life is not too challenging. In fact, we are very understanding of all who have problems, and we can help them through anything. Really? Do we really think we have all the answers? Then, boom, we are blaming God for this tragic event in our lives! We have been enjoying life because God has blessed us abundantly. Now do tragic events change how we live our faith? Christ refused to let us be casualties of sin and continuously experience tragedies and trauma! Our hearts and souls are suffering a great deal of pain; we can barely get out of bed; and when we do, our world looks very dark and hopeless. In good times we have faith and life is good. How can we keep our faith in God when hard, very hard times wipe us out? Thank God, Christ took His love to this: Greater love has no one than this, that someone lay down his life for his friends. (John 15:13) Which He did for each and every one of us!

Yes, tragedies happen; and yes, some are very traumatic; even so, life continues. Sadness and anger can be a part of our recovery or a part of our built-up stress and outrage. Our beautiful journey with Christ will continue, even through the trauma, when our faith is true, compassionately true!

In fact, while we might never forget this event, we can move on from it through our compassionate faith—a faith that is continuously in prayer and seeks a life of forgiveness. Sure, it is easy to say, nevertheless, so hard to live it—a life of forgiveness. Sometimes, we just want and choose to be sad or angry or both; yet, this is where we have our Savior, Jesus! Our faith in Him is to believe His testimony in the Bible. His love is real, and He can lead us out of dark days and into His light. First we must believe in His unconditional love.

He is our friend and will never forsake us. Living in His love always overcomes any darkness or pain in our lives. Let's seek His way!

Be completely humble and gentle; be patient, bearing with one another in love. (Ephesians 4:2)

Chapter 13
SEEKING V RUNNING

ONE DAY AS WE WERE WATCHING A LITTLE League baseball practice, we could hear the coach and his team working together. As the coach was hitting the ground balls to the different positions, by accident, we believe, he hit a little pop-up between the pitcher's mound and third base. Nobody moved; and, regretfully, the ball landed on the ground. The coach was very patient and asked the team what should have happened. All the players looked to him for the answer. He responded to this by asking a simple question, "In a real game who would try to catch this ball?" Again, no answer! The coach then realized a pitcher was not on the mound; therefore, maybe the team thought he would have caught the ball. The coach asks, "Are we a team that tries to be the best? Does this team hustle to catch a ball when it is hit?" The whole team roared, "Yeah, coach"! The coach with a very confident and trustful voice stated, "So if someone calls for the fly ball and can catch it while hustling to catch it then we would be doing the right thing, right"? Again, the team responded with an enthusiastic response; "Yeah coach"!

Thinking he had the team headed in the right direction, he hit another pop-up in front of the third baseman; but it was not very high, and there was no way the youngster would be able to catch it. Then the whole team heard this young man shout, "I ain't got it coach; I ain't got it", while he was running as fast as he could and giving his best trying to catch the ball! Is this what we do when facing life's hard times? We run knowing we cannot get away, or we just stand there waiting for something to happen because we do not know what to do or how to get through this situation. Then we find that God was there, and no matter what happens, He will be there! So now we run to Him, whether this situation is painful or joyful.

Yet, maybe we still are unsure; so, what should we do? How do we respond to this? Then comes the wouldas, shouldas, and what-just-happened thoughts. The land of doubt is where we are, and soon we will be falling further into a dark place. A sadness, maybe anger or shame take over because we did not keep running or seeking a place of love and hope. The young third baseman kept running even though he knew he would not be able to catch the ball because he listened to a voice that he trusted. He hustled because, as a child, there was no doubt, no anger, and no sadness on this team. This team worked at being there for each other because their coach was there for them. He never allowed them to be hard on each other or yell at someone for making a mistake. This is what we will receive from God when we listen to Him, when we learn to trust Him. Through thick or thin He is there. All we have to do is take the time to listen and begin to seek His way. Therefore, run to that love and peace we need so we can face life with confidence and, no matter what, trust God! For He will strengthen us, and we will find the way when we have confidence and trust in our Heavenly Father.

Ask and it will be given to you; seek, and you will find; knock, and it will opened to you. (Matthew 7:7)

Chapter 14
HE WILL STRENGTHEN ME

A YOUNG BOY WANTED TO LIVE LIFE, A JOYOUS life! Joey wanted his dad and mom to love him. He was 11 years old, and things just were not working out in a positive way, according to Joey. Neither school, nor athletics, nor his peers gave him any attention or feeling of belonging. When mom and dad would go out for the evening they would have a baby sitter, Linda, take care of him and his younger sister. Joey did build a nice relationship with Linda, and he learned to trust her. Soon Joey had his 12th birthday, and he was hoping for changes in his life—acceptance! You see, Joey was born with a club foot. Some surgeries had been performed on this, foot and he was just starting to walk without a significant limp. Joey was joyful and happy, kind to others, always accepting of the foul jokes about his limp. Joey only wanted others to be nice; significantly, he would go out of his way to help people and always with a smile.

One evening while his parents were out, Linda was babysitting Joey and his sister. His sister was in bed and had fallen asleep. Linda, 22 years old, stronger and bigger than Joey, took him into the basement and raped him. Joey was devastated, to say the least. Linda told him if he told anyone, she would make sure all the young men in his school would know that a woman had sex with him and he wanted to call it rape. Also, she might just do the same to him again or hurt his sister. Joey struggled to find a way to get rid of this hurt and ugliness that lingered over him. His smile went away, and so did his joy! He had been going to church with his mom and felt close with God; yet, how could the God he knew let this happen? This turmoil and extreme pain became a nightmare. Looking for ways to ease his pain and end his nightmares, he started to hang with the fun crowd—drug users and sellers. In a matter of months, Joey was using drugs that eased his pain, and soon he was selling drugs so he could buy more drugs. At 14 years old, Joey was arrested for possession of drugs. He was sent to a drug and alcohol unit for young men. It was there that he began to heal and disclose the root of his trauma—his anger and pain!

Joey began healing because he wanted smiles back in his life! He wanted to get back to experiencing the ups and downs of life through rose-colored glasses versus "Woes-colored" glasses. Joey was seeking to put back the smile on his face and his heart. He knew this would help him embrace the joys of life, while giving him the strength and courage to find a way through the difficult, painful times!

He told the supervisor of the Drug and Alcohol Treatment Unit that his life the past few years had been in turmoil, and that he wanted to find, once again, that heart that smiled and was at peace with God.

Joey stated that he heard in his initial D & A treatment/groups/AA/NA meetings that he needed a higher power. He wanted a way to heal and begin a life with love and peace at the center. His supervisor asked him, "What does Higher Power mean to you?" Joey's response was, "God, of course!" So Joey was on a new journey, the answer to his prayers. It was not easy, since he needed to unload what had happened to him. It was a heavy burden, and the nightmares were still happening. His fear that his sister could be harmed was overwhelming. Joey began this journey by telling his Mom and Dad about his trauma. Mom was angry—at the woman and Joey. She could not understand why Joey did not tell her about this when it happened! However, she began to calm down as Joey explained how Linda forcefully threatened harm to his little sister and had a very dangerous looking face—the same face she displayed while she was raping him.

Joey's mother saw the fear in his face as he disclosed the dread of this traumatic event and what would happen if he ever told anyone about it. Joey's Dad reacted just as Joey said he would—no emotion. Dad stated: "Is that what you wanted to tell me, is that it?" Joey's Dad had been through trauma too! He was a Vietnam veteran with buried secrets. Joey had witnessed many of Dad's moments of fear, anger, and hopelessness. While these moments had decreased in the past few years, they still influenced his Dad's processing of life's events. Dad's moments were real and very painful. The events that caused them were equally painful. Joey knew his Dad's processing was based on his past life and that he could not problem solve these events.

However, Joey did begin his journey and began forgiving all who had caused his pain. The nightmares did not ease up until his mother told him the baby sitter had been arrested for other crimes and was no longer in the area. Also, a letter was sent to his county's Children's Bureau stating what had happened. Joey no longer feared Linda getting to him or his sister because his Dad told him in a second family session that he and Joey together could take care of this person now that Joey was becoming a man. Joey stated that this did not mean he was rough and tough; rather, he was now able to work through his fears and let go of the past. God was now back in his life, and he had his smile back. Also, Joey wanted to help his Dad heal too!

Fear not, for I am with you; be not dismayed, for I am your God; I will strengthen you, I will help you, I will uphold you with my righteous right hand. (Isaiah 41: 10)

Chapter 15
YOU AND THOSE WHO ARE THERE FOR YOU

AS WE WERE DISCUSSING MARK'S LIFE, IT IS clear how he found joy, peace, love, and mercy without looking for it. His life was full of vices—sin at a very young age. He was looking for ways to get high, which is what everyone else was doing, according to Mark. He was 12 years old; and he just wanted to get high. Many of his friends were using marijuana. It looked like fun. Plus, he had heard older kids talk about it—another reason he had to try it. From this time on, Mark lived for this type of fun and would risk getting in trouble to get his high. In fact, when he was old enough to join the Army at 18 he enlisted because he would be able to go to Germany where hashish was inexpensive, very easy to get, and of a much higher quality. He was on his way to a life of "fun through drugs".

This life of fun started to go the wrong way shortly after he was discharged from the service. In order to get his marijuana, Mark had to purchase it through people no one would want to take home and to meet the family.

Mark had a good job, and all was fine until his illicit drug use took him down the road of trouble—violent people became his friends! Now he was one of them and would do what it took to make sure all his fellow dealers and drugs were protected from other dealers who would try to muscle in on their territory. Then it happened—one of his violent cohorts was murdered over drugs and Mark wanted revenge! He was furious! Mark was fuming; and, after burying his fellow drug dealer/user, it was time to even the playing field: some one had to pay and Mark was about to make this happen. There would be no negotiations, no apologies. Just an eye-for-an eye and a-tooth-for-a-tooth plan! It was time to pay his fellow dealers a visit and get even!

Then Mark had a vision: a visitor told him revenge would fix nothing, and he needed to change his ways and the people involved with his life. Though Mark did not understand what was happening, he did not complete his intent to murder someone. Mark continued to have episodes that challenged his way of thinking and living. He struggled to understand what was going on and how these changes made sense. Yet he began to change, gradually and with resistance. You see, Mark liked his life-style; in fact, he struggled against this change. Soon Mark realized his wants were changing. He would try to use marijuana and alcohol to get high, but they no longer had the desired effects, and the desire was diminishing rapidly. Mark discovered that his old way of life was being replaced by something, but he could not figure out what this new way was and how it came about.

Mark's future was now in the hands of something or someone; yet, he could not figure out what the reasons were for this change. Mark, like Saul, knew about God; and that was all; he knew about God. Like Saul, Mark lived a life he wanted and desired without any repercussions; both were above any laws! Like Paul, Mark changed because of divine intervention.

What indications do we have that suggest Mark's story had this intervention? The answer is: Mark did not want to change; he did not understand how this would help him. Is this not the same thinking many of the previous people mentioned in this book? We can change because we want to change or even if we do not. And both take God's hand to be involved. "With God all things are possible." (Matthew 19:26). Mark became a solid Christian and he reached out to many people who needed intervention in some way. He would help veterans, single moms, children of parents who were in prison, and the list continues. His smile is one that displays a love for God, which Mark shares with us, you and me.

This is the day the Lord has made; We will rejoice and be glad in it! (Psalm 118:24)

Chapter 16
Should I change my Name to Job?

Hi, my name is Danny; and I am a fun kind of guy. I have been having fun for a good while now. I am all of 33 years of age; man life has been great! You see I cannot sit still—I NEED TO HAVE FUN! I never miss work, no matter what. I have gone without sleep many times. Girls! They all love me! Alcohol! It's a big part of my life, as well as other drugs! Man, am I having fun. Oh, yeah, now there is heroin that is cheap and powerful! Wow! Now I am really having fun!

This was happening about ten years ago; and then, one Sunday evening, after partying throughout the weekend, I think I was driving home and apparently I was in a car wreck. I did not wake up for 3 days. All the while, I was in the hospital being treated for multiple wounds. At that very moment, I was wishing I could go back in time. My body was hurting all over, especially my knees and back. Also, I needed a fix and some booze; that would cheer me up, as it always did. Where's everyone? I need to party!

Then they showed up, the doctors and nurses; the news was not good. My left knee was beyond repair! Also, I had more stitches then I could count all over my back and other leg. The pain was almost unbearable. All I need is a good hit! My pain will be gone, and we can party! No one would listen; they kept saying, "Calm down".

Here I sit about 10 years after the accident, and I am not doing so good. I am now going on 43 years old, and I feel like I am much older. Plus, I cannot work anymore; and my wife is at her wits' end because all I ever do is hurt. During my first visit to the hospital, I unknowingly received a staph infection. It has now damaged my immune system, which means my body is extremely limited in fighting off infections of any kind. I am now on a super antibiotic due to an infection that started in my right leg and spread rapidly. I have consistently been on and off antibiotics over these past years. The viruses seem to get stronger; thus, I have to take stronger antibiotics. Recently, the surgeons took out my left knee replacement and replaced it with a plastic spacer (temporarily for 6 weeks). The doctors believed the virus had become a super virus and would hide in the metal knee replacement when antibiotics were injected into my body to destroy the virus. It was a very painful procedure which proved unsuccessful. I eventually lost my left leg above the knee due to the second knee replacement exploding inside my leg. The doctors did an emergency amputation to stop the arterial bleeding and save my life.

I now have lost my right leg just below the knee, due to an infection that started in my right foot/ankle area and began spreading rapidly up my leg. The antibiotics were ineffective as it spread; hence, to save some of my leg, an emergency amputation was ordered. These past ten years I have spent hundreds of days in the hospital. Most of these days were due to emergency surgery because an infection had started to attack an organ. Follow-up tests after open heart surgery due to a heart attack indicated my arteries were not functioning.

Since my health was failing, the doctors believed my body needed more help than just the antibiotics; so my body was inoculated with steroids. These years of treatment weakened my skeletal system; hence, I have had to deal with broken bones and dislocated joints endlessly! In fact, it was the cause of the infections in both of my legs. Both of my shoulders are in need of surgery because the joints are disintegrating while my neck vertebrae are in need of surgery to correct the alignment so there is not constant pain from the vertebrae pinching my spine. The doctors, as well as my family and I, are worried if I have any further surgery. Will I heal internally and externally? My system is failing more and more. Should I change my name to Job?

I, also, have a cyst forming in my brain which is starting to cause headaches, sometimes severe. What am I to do? I cannot go through surgery without assurance it will heal! However, I have and will always have Jesus because He gave it all for me! While Danny has asked, "Should I change my name to Job"? he is not going to turn from Jesus! Sure, he gets angry; and sure, he would like his physical life to be much better; however, Danny knows he can get through each day by staying focused on Jesus. It does not matter how his days are physically! What matters is how his whole being is, and only Jesus can make the difference in each and every day. Danny's truth is just this: I cannot change who I am or how I am physically by taking a pill or a shot. I can only change who I am and how I feel physically by following the way Christ has shown me—through His Word—the Bible!

When Danny blamed others (doctors, work, drugs, etc.) for his conditions, he became angry and unforgiving. This led to a downward spiral of darkness and fear! He wanted to die! Where did his love for Christ go? A better question to ask: How was his love for Jesus taken from him? When asked Danny would say: "All I have is pain and more pain! How can you even ask me that question?" Danny changed this downward spiral rather quickly though. He did this because he felt totally alone, and he knew nothing on earth could change his condition, nothing! Danny accepted this while letting his whole being find the love of his Savior, Jesus, as the answer. Danny has lived for 10 more years; although his physical health has worsened, Danny only asks he be able to share Jesus with others. "Nothing but the blood of Jesus can change your life." He continues his life as a man named Danny, a child of our Heavenly Father!

Then Job answered the Lord and said: I know that You can do everything, and that no purpose of Yours can be withheld from you. You asked, "Who is this who hides counsel without knowledge?" Therefore I have uttered what I did not understand, things too wonderful for me, which I did not know. Listen, please, and let me speak; You said, "I will question you, and you shall answer me." "I have heard of You by the hearing of the ear, but now my eye sees You. Therefore I abhor myself, and repent in dust and ashes." (Job 42:1—6)

Now the Lord blessed the latter days of Job more than his beginning. (Job 42:12)

Chapter 17
SERVITUDE ATTITUDE: HEALING BEGINS WITH SERVING

How do you go about serving the Lord without disrupting our church's role in the community? Or, how do you go about doing our Savior's work without offending others? What should you do when your family turns their backs to you because you are not following their religious and/or cultural ways? Which service for your church magnifies our Lord? Who should direct your commitment to the Lord? The who, where, what, and hows are not, apparently, our Lord and Savior. Our Savior states in John 13:34—35: "A new commandment I give to you, that you love one another, just as I have loved you, you also are to love one another. By this, all people will know that you are my disciples, if you have love for one another." Do we Christians love one another?

Well let's ask God how to continue in serving Him or maybe, we ask this from a religious point of view. Should we seek knowledge from Gandhi or Dalai Lama? Let's review Gandhi's statement: "I do like Jesus ,but it is the Christians I have a problem with." This might sound very critical of our faith in Christ; on the contrary, a servitude attitude (God is first and we are his servants) begins with God, Jesus and the Holy Spirit. However, when we suffer a tragedy, we question how God has answered our prayers. The our doubt results in our lack of servitude.

We have become <u>blamers</u>, and now we seek permission from man to serve God.We are damaged because we have been broken due to our own choices. Now, we allow man's way to guide us; as we continue to be <u>blamers</u>! We cannot do this because someone could be offended or we cannot do that because it is too risky, etc. "If any of you lacks wisdom, let him ask of God, who gives to all liberally and without reproach, and it will be given to him. But let him ask in faith, with no doubting, for he who doubts is like a wave of the sea driven and tossed by the wind." *(James 2:5-6)* God wants us to step up to the plate and go for it! Not to hit a home run or strike out. He just wants us to trust Him and let Jesus show us the way. Which is, by the way, more than a home run, even a grand slam, a World Series, a Super Bowl, a Stanley Cup and any other thing this world has to offer.

So instead of being a <u>blamer</u> let's look at being a <u>completer</u>! We do this by seeking Him through His word and living out His word. Being <u>completers</u> does not and must not be compared to revolting, being displeased, or living contrary to our Bible based Christian Faith. In fact, this is how we are to live and be lights to His world—by being <u>completers:</u> going to college campuses and walking the streets to be completely truthful with people about our Savior, going to nursing homes and sharing His Word with residents, along with their families, giving them hope, or going to a dementia unit with the peace and love of Christ helps the residents find some calming. There are people who need help with monthly bills; we can help there through our local food banks. There are widows who cannot take care of their properties, and the list goes on, and on…. The <u>blamers</u> state, "Let their families or government take care of them!" The worst excuse is: "We can't go out to colleges or onto streets because some in government believe it unconstitutional due to their view of the constitution." This question can answer that: "Then how do professors of the colleges and universities get away with discrediting our Christian Faith?

Have we put our faith/lights under baskets, and are we no longer shining in this country or anywhere else? Did the founding fathers of America put their faith/lights under baskets? Or did they risk their lives to save their right to serve Christ? Read true history, and you will find the meaning of laying down your life for a friend! America was founded by Christians, people who wanted God involved in all our lives through our Christian Faith! Thus, we should be doing the same in order to help the needy and save people for an eternal life with our Heavenly Father and our Savior Jesus Christ.

But be doers of the word, and not hearers only, deceiving yourselves. For if anyone is a hearer of the word and not a doer, he is like a man observing his natural face in a mirror; for he observes himself, goes away, and immediately forgets what kind of man he was. But he who looks into the perfect law of liberty and continues in it, and is not a forgetful hearer but a doer of the work, this one will be blessed in what he does. (James 1:23-25)

Chapter 18
STARTING THE JOURNEY HOME

WILL IS A MAN WHO HAS ACQUIRED A GREAT deal of wisdom. Some has come from his childhood, some from his time in the military, some from his experiences in his work, but most comes from the time he spent serving the Lord. Will's father was an alcoholic and did not have much to do with Will's life as a young man. Because Will's father's alcoholism impacted him so negatively while he was growing up, Will did not let alcohol enter his home and work life. Then at the age of 17 he joined the US Navy and served four years during the Korean War, the Forgotten War. Will was very proud of his Navy commitment and had many great stories that he shared with other veterans. However, Will's time in the Navy was spent in airplanes rather than a ship. He traveled around the world, spending time in Japan, Alaska, all over the western and eastern coasts of the USA. He flew over some of Asia, which included Korea.

Upon his return home to western Pennsylvania, Will learned a trade that involved heating and air conditioning. Will eventually started his own heating and air conditioning company. Throughout this part of his life, Will was not close with God. He knew of God; however, he did not know God. Then God showed up in his life.

Will sensed something was not right with his life. His business was having way too many financial challenges. He was, also, experiencing difficulties within his family and felt his friends weren't being supportive. Then Will began seeking peace and joy the way a

Christian would seek it through Jesus Christ. Feeling a huge hole in his life, he felt he'd lost all direction! Will then cried out to God in a completely truthful and humble manner. He was compassionate in his reaching out for God; then God showed up. Will experienced a prayer moment: he received the Holy Spirit and cried tears, tears and more tears of joy! He felt his whole body being cleansed! Although the business took some time to turn around and become prosperous through hard work and being diligent, his family/personal life was still challenging; but Will had given his life to Christ, and he could move through anything that this world demanded.

As Will's life continued, his faith became stronger, allowing him to deal with two traumatic events in his life. His oldest son had ridden motorcycles for many years and at the age of 32 years a deer ran into him. Will found out later that his son's wreck ended far off the road. Severely injured and in a great deal of pain, he was pinned under his huge Harley-Davidson motorcycle. Then Will found out that his son had taken his life due to the severe pain he experienced while the hot motorcycle was lying on him burning him.

Will also witnessed his beautiful Christian wife, Vickie, go through a great deal of pain due to acute arthritis. The pain had become so severe that Vickie began treatment for it. Both Vickie and Will had been warned that the treatment could cause cancer. Unfortunately, it did! A little over a year after losing his son, Will also lost his dear and sweet wife of 35 years to cancer. Will's life was upside down! His sadness was immense! Sometimes his life seemed to be in a deep fog. All the same, Will knew where to find the peace and joy to heal his heart: take it to the Lord of all! Will began to visit folks in the nursing home where his wife had been a patient. Many of them were on hospice care, and their families were in need of the same hope that Will had received through our Savior. Since the time of his wife's passing, Will still visits this home once a week: he is 85 years old and continues to share his joy in serving the Lord with the patients and their families.

For He has rescued us from the dominion of darkness and brought us into the kingdom of the Son He loves, in whom we have redemption, the forgiveness of sins. (Colossians 1:13-14)

Chapter 19

LOVE DOES NOT BEHAVE RUDELY, DOES NOT SEEK ITS OWN, IS NOT EASILY ANGERED, THINKS NO EVIL, DOES NOT REJOICE IN INIQUITY BUT REJOICES IN TRUTH!

SO FAR, WE HAVE READ ABOUT MICK, JOSEPH, Charlie, Joey, Paul, Danny, Jimmy, Johnny and Will. Each person had experienced times of trauma. Yet, each one was able to find a way to heal. Yes, each one found a way to God—His love and His way!

A young lady, Anne, grew up with a mother May who would not give or accept love. May was about one person—herself! Even May's own mother (Anne's grandmother, Millie) was very torn over May's behavior. Anne spent her weeknights and weekends cleaning the house throughout the school year; and, if Anne's work was not good enough for May, then Anne would have to do it again. By the time Anne was 14 years old, she was also doing most of the cooking. May usually had an excuse for not doing the household chores—she was either ill or angry with someone.

While this would make most female teenagers angry and downright rebellious, Anne a loving heart for both her Fathers—God and her Dad! Each and every day she would tell both how much she loved them. This magnificent love enabled Anne to feel and show this love for her three siblings, also.

When Anne turned 18 and graduated from high school she moved out because of her mother. Anne found a job and supported herself. Then, when she visited home to see her Dad and her three siblings, her mother would make her clean the house and cook on Saturdays. After six months of this she moved back home and continued taking care of the house, although it was never a home for her. Watching her mother mistreat her Dad and her brothers on a daily basis made these days very upsetting. Anne was able to reach out to her grandmother, Millie, and her aunts. While Anne did have happy times with them and her siblings, she was never joyous or at peace, especially at her home.

At the age of 22, Anne, however, found love and married Barry. Barry drew close to her Dad and they developed a protective relationship so Anne would be safe from her mother's anger. However, several people warned Barry that no one liked May because of her abusive behavior! Soon after Barry and Anne were married May wanted control of their marriage, so Anne would visit her Dad when May was not around. During holidays, Anne made the visits home sweet to Dad and short to May. Anne soon had two boys who were loved by their grandfather. Nonetheless, May stated: "I am not going to be a baby sitter. You had them so you can take care of them." Neighbors and her mother-in-law would baby sit on occasions, but Anne never asked May.

One could ask: "Was May's behavior devastating to Anne"? It was not; Anne knew what love was through our Almighty Father. She knew the kind of love that a mother and a wife should give. Her devotion to the Father was as He asked: "Above all these put on love, which binds everything together in perfect harmony." *(Colossians 3:14)* Anne had found joy and peace through her love for the Father.

Her Dad passed away at 58 years old. While this saddened her, Anne knew God was in charge, and this too would pass. Dad was with the Lord and free of all the pain the world had unloaded on him. It did not stop there. Anne was told to be at May's house the day after her Dad's funeral. When Anne met with her three siblings and May, the first thing May stated was, "Anne, you are out of the will." When Anne asked, "Is that it?" May answered with a stern, "Yes". Anne left and never returned. Soon after this episode, Barry asked Anne to try to make amends with May. Barry was told gently, "I have a mother, your mom has been a mother to me ever since I first met her. Your Mom always displays her love for God and others. I just feel so loved by Mom."

Anne went through life always caring for others. When their sons were almost teenagers, Anne and Barry became foster parents of a five-day-old premature baby boy weighing less than five pounds. Anne and her family soon bonded with this child from God. Because he was premature and an alcohol syndrome baby, Anne checked on him throughout the night for the first several months. Initially, the baby's biological mother had little contact with her son, visiting only twice during the first year. Then, suddenly, overnight visits were ordered; during the next few months, prior to his third birthday, the overnights began. His visits were from Friday evening to Monday morning. On his third birthday Anne received the devastating news that the child would be going back with his biological mother. Two weeks after his third birthday the child was taken from Anne and her family.

Anne did not give up on God because she knew "Anything is possible with God" (Matthew 19:26). Anne had experienced grief, but she let her pain be soothed by our Savior. Then Anne reentered the work force as a cashier at a nearby store. Many people soon experienced a Godly person and knew if they went through her line they would be treated kindly and honestly. People would chat with her, especially those who had lost trust with mankind.

Sadly, Anne passed several years later; and at the funeral home, many people came to let her family know how much she was missed. Many visitors were customers from the store where they experienced her beautiful smile. Many of these people were not aware of the loss of her Dad, whom she loved dearly, and the fragile yet loving foster child of 3 years. None knew of her regretful and unloving rearing by a woman who had tormented her all of her life. She always presented herself as a caring and smiling lady of God. Yes, she cried when saddened by her losses; however, she was always thankful for the many blessings she had received from our Heavenly Father.

Let all that you do be done in love. (1 Corinthians 16:14)

Chapter 20

SOFTLY AND GENTLY SHARING GOD

TRAUMATIC EVENTS HAPPEN IN ALL OF OUR lives. We are a fallen people and we have a Heavenly Father; so we can begin the healing process through Him, though some might say, "Nope, no way"! So much of our culture directs us to finding ways of emotional and spiritual healing through some worldly comfort. Does this really happen? Can this really happen? While we have hope and want to overcome our hurt, what comfort do we find in our own follies of happiness? You will find no greater love than God's love for us. He had His only Son lay down His life for each and every one of us. Still, we desire to seek man's ways of healing from traumatic events.

Consider Peter, the one who stated he would never let his friend and Savior, Jesus, be taken away. He even severed a soldier's ear with a sword! Then Peter watched as they tortured and crucified our Lord. I can only image the trauma this caused him.

Then consider Paul, who as Saul, had followers of Jesus murdered! Hunting them down, causing them to go into hiding, Saul became renowned; among his peers he was a hero! Then he met Jesus on his way to Damascus. Saul became a changed man and began a new life of servitude versus his old life of self-gratitude. Saul sought selfish ideals, a worldly reverence! Now he was a man who would serve his Savior by sharing his love of God with those who still feared him as Saul. Because they fear recurring trauma, many people today feel they can never trust again . This world will only cause more suffering, more pain, and more fear. This fear is magnified through our emotions, our thought process, and our unforgiveness.

A second child is born into a very loving family. The first child is doing well and is very healthy, into everything and anything. Mom and Dad are constantly on their toes. However, the second son is born with some frailties and illnesses, suffering from difficulties in swallowing and breathing. So Mom and Dad develop fears which are displayed to the child. As he matures to eight years of age, he is diagnosed with asthma which requires treatment via a nebulizer and medication. Also, he has food allergies. During his formative years, he was allowed to eat anywhere and could eat at his own pace just as long as he ate. His behavior was in no way to be challenged.

By being defiant and manipulative he developed a life that was going to be lived his way. His parents began trying to correct his behaviors. He overheard his nurses, doctors and parents stating that his asthma could lead to severe problems if he did not do what he was told to do, i.e., use the nebulizer and medication. He was experiencing behavioral modification through fear, and his fear was now that he would die! This also became a tool for him to use on others when anger, sadness, or anxiety became predominant. "You are so mean to me, I hope you die!" This was one of his many fear-driven responses to any correction he received. His fears led him to be very nasty to anyone opposing him, resulting in more aggressive and self-destructive behavior. He was afraid to be alone because he might die! So devastating to a parent to hear this kind of speech from an eight-year-old! Yet when he attended school he did well.

Right away most people want to judge and not be judged! How do we help this child overcome his fears? In his mind, this is life, and this is how I am going to live it; so leave me alone because I don't like you, and I hope you die! His fears dictate his view of life. What are his fears? Who instilled these fears in him?

Or the better questions are: Is he doing this for attention? Are the parents now trying to correct him and hold him accountable? Are his thoughts full of fear—losing his freedom to do what he wants, when he wants, and using psychic trauma on anyone he thinks is trying to take this away from him? These are fears full of anger, almost to a place of rage. He acts sad and scared, while inside he is conniving more ways to get what he wants! When called on these behaviors, he acts sad and scared again, and again, and again. If the family wants to go out to dinner, he is too tired; and he convinces Mom that he cannot go out. Mom believes him, and soon he is back on track to get what he wants: if I can't have the fun I want, then neither will you. However, Dad states; "We are going out and so are you." The boy starts to cry, but the Dad stays strong, and the family goes out to dinner. Soon at the restaurant, all is well, and each of the children is doing well. When back at the house, the neighbors visit; and everyone is outside having fun, with no one being tired.

When parents give in to their own fear and anxiety their children will use this against them. Children cry out for boundaries. When none are provided due to fear and/or anxiety what takes place? Crying, yelling, fighting, cheating, and the list goes on and on!

Jill wants to raise her family in a loving and caring environment and strives to do this by giving almost her entire waking hours to her children (3 girls): laundry, cleaning the house, taking the girls to appointments, and all their activities, so on and so on. Where is the husband? Doug works a lot of hours each week; yet, when he is home, he helps with the laundry, the cooking, the cleaning. This happens even though he works six days a week, at least 12 hour shifts. All you hear from Jill is how tired she is and how her work is never done. While Doug does help, Jill always reacts negatively to how he corrects the children. He is not tough enough here, too tough there. She will even go as far as stating: "The oldest one, Cindy, is so brash and always has an answer! She never ever listens to anything I say." Then when Cindy is creating a moment of chaos with her younger sister, Bobbi, Jill will yell at her. The youngest, Linda, has to hear this and knows that yelling will occur all day. Yet, Jill thinks she is creating a loving home.

How does all this yelling and constant on-edge life-style as a Mother begin? Did Jill's fears begin at home? Was her anxiety reinforced through her studies in college? Was she told by the so-called professionals that correcting children with negative consequences would only hurt the child, the proof being: just look how you turned out with all this anxiety and fear instilled in you!

Yeah, that is what the professionals believe; and you dare not challenge them because they will make your life as a college student miserable. Why do they do this? Their answers are always the same: "My negative upbringing is the reason I do these things!" This is the most ridiculous excuse for their behaviors. These professionals were corrected for wrongdoing and could not get away with the negativity they were creating. Their anxiety and fears continue to allow them to play the victim card. Do no harm to the child; let her find her way, and so the "do no harm" continues until the child is out of control. Consequently it must be a mental health problem requiring medication. So we end up giving our children pills and more pills.

How did we get here? Where did this nonsense begin? When did this nonsense begin? The answer is simple—we are all fallen people. There is no way around it. We look for answers from our fallen mentors. Take the loving approach: God loves us and wants us to share His love for us with others; therefore, God corrects us through His kindness and His truthfulness. He is the only consistent being in our lives. He will always be there, no matter what! We as parents strive to always be there for our children. As our heavenly Father shows us the right way to walk through life, we are to do this with our children.

God gives us boundaries to follow all through our lives—the Bible. Hence, we will give our children boundaries too. We apply these boundaries with love, and not with yelling or threats. God does not do that, so we shall not either. If a child does not follow the rules then the child will face the logical consequences. When a parent does this the child is being prepared for life. Giving in to the child's wants does not help the child mature. Even then some will fail; however, the parents who apply boundaries give them the tools to seek God in all they do. Consider a child who is continuously misbehaving at home: mean to his siblings, questioning all his parents requests, not doing chores, not following directions, lying, cheating, and causing anxiety.

However, when in school, this child excels and does follow directions. Also, there are no attention seeking behaviors. Reason? Boundaries have been set, and this child has seen there were consequences for misbehavior—detention, not being able to participate in recess, etc. These are followed through, so the child knows it will not be fun or easy to manipulate the school's teachers and administrators. What does this prove? Boundaries work! Follow-up works! Consequences work!

Let's take a more in-depth look at this child though. Some professionals will ask, where is your research to back this "philosophy"? Or how does your religion work when science says otherwise? The proof is this: our society prospers because of the people who know right from wrong. People who understand the gift of love know it will persevere because they will strive to be righteous and not tolerate those who try to manipulate or bully. The love in Godly people creates respect for others. Kindness will persevere and has persevered throughout the ages. This is all the proof one needs that setting boundaries and following through with consequences does indeed work. God's love never fails; however, we do and will continue to fail. Yet, He forgives us each and every time. Try this as a parent: show the way, provide the right path with boundaries and consequences, forgive and forget each episode, reinforce the correct behaviors, and watch your child grow without all the fears and anxieties.

And now these three remain: faith, hope, and love. But the greatest of these is love. (1 Corinthians 13:13)

Final Chapter

COMPASSIONATE TRUTHFULNESS IS POSSIBLE WHEN PEOPLE ARE TRUTHFUL AND TRUSTWORTHY TO OTHERS AND THEMSELVES

WE TRY TO DO OUR BEST WHEN WE ARE AT WORK, church, a store, a community function, and sports events. What are the reasons we do this? Because we want others to think we are nice, kind, hardworking, good people? Maybe we want to think we are kind, nice, hardworking, good people? Could it be we are trying to teach our family to be kind, nice, hardworking, good people? Or we think we can get into heaven if we are kind, good, and nice people? If this is where we are at and all the above is true, then we are only fooling ourselves and no one else! You see, being Compassionately Truthful starts with yourself!

We hear all the time about how to be successful by following this plan or that plan or etc., etc.; and, without hesitation, we begin to think about our losses: how we have failed, how the guy down the street made it and we are better than he; or she landed this great job, and I know how she got it; my oh my, I would never do that. Being human, when times of unhappiness hit us, we have to blame someone else or God! These are not desperate times we are talking about—rather, just everyday happenings. I did not get the raise I deserve, or my daughter is better than Cindy's daughter in basketball; yet, she starts while my daughter never gets to play. My spouse is not staying in shape, and my buddy's wife is. How lucky he is! I bought this car, and it has been nothing but trouble. Yet my goofball of a brother-in-law's truck has never seen the inside of a service station, except for an oil change or tires. Some guys have all the luck! On and on and on we go. Blaming here and blaming there. Questioning, questioning, and we end each day this way: When am I going to rewarded?

My question is: Who do we think we are? When and where and how and why do we flame the blame? To answer all these questions, one must look for wisdom, wisdom from God!

"For the Lord gives wisdom; From His mouth comes knowledge and understanding; He stores up sound wisdom for the upright; He is a shield to those who walk uprightly; He guards the paths of justice, and preserves the way of His saints. Then you will understand righteousness and justice, equity and every good path. When wisdom enters your heart, and knowledge is pleasant to your soul, discretion will preserve you; understanding will keep you, to deliver you from the way of evil, from the man who speaks perverse things, from those who leave the paths of uprightness." (Proverbs 2:6-13). Where does it say wisdom and happiness go together? Where do you read: when one is wise he will be happy? The definition of happiness is a feeling that comes over you when you know life is good and you can't help but smile. A sense of well-being, joy, and contentment, when people are successful, or safe, or lucky; thus, they feel happy. Wisdom begins when one seeks it and has "The Fruit of the Spirit: love, joy peace, long-suffering, patience, kindness, goodness, faithfulness, gentleness, and self control." (Galatians 5:22-23). Their wisdom is from God, and He provides us with a "joyful" heart. When a neighbor's fortune allows them to purchase a new car or their daughter is doing well with her singing lessons; (in fact, she is singing at church next Sunday), they are happy, for now. That is what happiness is—temporary.So if your neighbor loses his job then loses his car, will he be happy? Of course not! Or if his daughter can't sing at their church because of stage-fright, happy? Of course not! Will there be anger and frustrations in their house? Yes, of course, and their answer will be: Would you be happy if these things happened to you? I paid a lot of money for my daughter's singing lessons and that car. I am angry, and deservedly so! Then throw losing my job into the pile of my undoings, and I become furious! Or when we see a woman grieving because she lost her husband and is enveloped by loneliness. She is very sad and frustrated wondering how she will ever make it without him. Or a neighbor's wife passes, and he is a mess. He doesn't know how to pay the bills or wash his clothes or cook, etc., etc.; and he is not just sad and lonely, he is frustrated. Losing someone is hard, especially when you shared God's joyous days!

The difference between happiness and joy is: people who lose their temporary happiness compounded by stress will be angry and have flames of blame. One who has a joyful heart will be sad because of his losses but still seeks God's guidance through this temporary sadness. For their Fruit of the Spirit will guide them back to peace, love, goodness, faithfulness, gentleness, self-control, and long-suffering. Their joy is deep and will keep any attacks of losses temporary, not allowing the world to provoke them to sadness or allowing conceit and blame to take over their everyday lives. The long-suffering is acceptable because of their joyful spirit. This does not mean they won't suffer from losses of jobs or spouses, but their wounds will be soothed by their faith, self-control, gentleness, and goodness. They are filled with a compassion for the truth: God's Word! This is how we can complete the journey of hope and love for those who suffer severe episodes of violence, losses, and injuries. We guide through the Fruit of the Spirit. We share our joy with them while God enters into their lives, and they find His joy. The only way to do this is to be completely and compassionately truthful.

> *Therefore, having been justified by faith, we have peace with God through our Lord Jesus Christ, through whom also we have access by faith into this grace in which we stand, and rejoice in hope of the glory of God. And not only that, but we also glory in tribulations, knowing that tribulation produces perseverance, and perseverance, character; and character, hope. Now hope does not disappoint, because the love of God has*

been poured out in our hearts by the Holy Spirit who was given to us. (Romans 5:1-5)

A Light Has Come On, and It Is in Me Through Him, Our Savior

Here is my heart, Lord
Help me to keep it joyful
Always seeking You and only You
You show how to be hopeful

I have been under a basket
I hide from my light
You placed in me and for me
I chose to keep it out of sight

Yet now You speak to my heart
And only truthfulness can be heard
For You speak truth and only truth
Through the Holy Spirit's word

My heart becomes overwhelmed with joy
I want to stay awake and keep this peace
Yet as I lay down at the end of the day
Night comes and I see my joy cease

It is not You Oh Lord, Oh how I know
For I am weak and You are strong
So I pray and Your truthful Words are heard
I am with you during days that are long,

Compassionately Truthful

Always and forever I will be with you
Compassionately Truthful, for you are
And always will be mine, for I created
You in my Image, just like the Star
That was over my Glorious Son

My prayers always end with: through Your Son and my Savior Jesus I ask and worship You for you are the One True God, an Awesome God! The God of Joy, Peace, Mercy, Hope, Love, and Grace. Forever more. Amen

> *Now after Jesus was born in Bethlehem of Judea in the days of Herod the king, behold, wise men from the East came to Jerusalem, saying, "Where is He who has been born King of the Jews? For we have seen His* STAR *in the East and have come to worship Him." (Matthew 2:1-2)*

> *And behold, an angel of the Lord stood before them, and the glory of the Lord shone around them, and they were greatly afraid. Then the angel said to them, "Do not be afraid, for behold I bring you good tidings of great joy which will be to all people. For there is born to you this day in the city of David a Savior who is Christ the Lord". (Luke 2: 9-11)*

www.ingramcontent.com/pod-product-compliance
Ingram Content Group UK Ltd.
Pitfield, Milton Keynes, MK11 3LW, UK
UKHW041949230426
12048UKWH00008B/224

9 781662 818226